Grief & Growth

Leigh Gembus

Copyright © 2017 Leigh Gembus

All rights reserved.

ISBN: 0648039404
ISBN-13: 978-0648039402

DEDICATION

This book is dedicated to women:

To the woman who raised me.

To the woman who broke me.

To the woman who loves me.

CONTENTS

Preface   i

GRIEF

1	Denial	9
2	Bargaining	36
3	Anger	51
4	Depression	73
5	Acceptance	92

GROWTH

6	Learn	113
7	Reboot	133
8	Action	145
9	Defining	159
10	Motivate	173
11	Align	189
12	Reflect	210

PREFACE

This book is a collection of poems that I wrote from 2013 to 2015. During this time, my life underwent a complete overhaul; with the catalyst being unexpected and unwelcome. From this change, it took everything that I thought I knew and believed about love, relationships, people and life and erased it.

I lost my motivation to do anything; I would do the bare minimum that I needed to to survive – work and attempt to eat and sleep – and repeat it day after day. There seemed to be no reason to get up in the morning and keep living.

I turned to writing to extract the thoughts and emotions that were inside me. I found it to be quite therapeutic; it allowed me to quantify and clarify what I was experiencing, which helped me to be more at ease with everything.

As I began to understand the new version of myself, I came to realise that many people have been through similar experiences. The pain that I was feeling was not unique and that many people, after experiencing trauma, are broken and are never able to pick up the pieces of their lives. They go on living as a ghostly version of themselves and no longer engage in their life, the world around them or investing in their wellbeing.

Once I picked myself up from my lowest point and developed into the person I am today, I realised how beneficial a helping hand and some information would have been whilst searching for some direction and meaning in the aftermath of the traumatic events. From the discovery of my values – PIA (Passion, Integrity, Authenticity) and HULK (Honesty, Understanding, Love and Kindness) – I knew that I had to share my experiences with others; to provide the assistance that I so desperately desired at the time. If I can help at least one person, then my pain would have been worth something.

Some of the works contained in this book are based on my actual experiences. They are not written and shared to point blame at anyone or bring discomfort. I have shared these pieces simply to help express the emotions and thoughts I experienced so that others may relate and discover that they too are not alone. They are in no way intended to bring pain to any other person.

I hope that upon reading this anthology of my poems that it gives you some motivation and inspiration to be present in your life once more; and that if there are times that it all seems too much, that there is hope and that there is always someone who will listen, you just have to speak out.

GRIEF

DENIAL

Hold You

Lost all energy
I have no fight.
There's only one thing
That will make this right;
If I can hold you
In my arms tonight
I'll never let go,
I'll hold you tight.

Changes

I reached for my lover,
I reached for my friend.
In the depths of darkness,
I'll do it again.

No longer here now, no longer the same,
Stop and wait here, each and every day.
Come on right back now, talk to my face,
A new life, a new love, it can be replaced.

I know you're different, I know that you've changed,
Just like I have, we are one and the same.
No denying the bond, the connection it's true,
The twists and the turns, led me straight back to you.

A heart full of hope, a mind full of dreams,
Right now it's different; not as it seems.
I hope it changes, comes right around,
The hopes and the dreams become the here and the now.

I keep this all quiet, you won't hear a word,
What happens, will happen; it has to occur.
But please know this, for it's true –
Through all of these changes,
I still love you.

Persist

Perhaps the fact you know they exist
Will be enough to let your love persist
Until one day you're in their arms;
When love can no longer
Bring you pain, or harm.

Knock

With my heart torn out
Thrown on the floor
I turned my back on love.

I cried and said – NO MORE!

Sat on my own
No more sadness to be dealt.
Until I heard that knock at the door.

Linger

Those wicked words escaped your lips and
In that moment was when my heart did break;
They shall echo in my mind forever more.

Lies in her Eyes

I tried looking in her eyes
As she turned quickly away.
No words spoken – saved me the lies
Right then I knew – my heart was betrayed.

Smoke

I compiled for you a list,
Of all the ways you'd opened my eyes;
The ways in which you'd changed my life.

When I showed you,
You laughed as you asked –
"What's this?"
As if my words were a joke.

As everything we built
Went down in flames;
It disappeared in selfish smoke.

Stars

So quiet –
No TV. No radio.
Just me and my guitar.
The laughs have stopped
The night is still;
I wonder where you are.
The room is cold
No stories to be told;
Never knew it would be this hard.

House is empty.
Bed is cold.
All that's left
Is the moon and stars.

Five Words

"*Of course* I love you…"
She proclaimed.
As if the stressed prefix
Made it real.

Never

I placed my love
Inside an open chest;
Containing an empty heart
And an ice cold soul.

Yet, I never thought
It would sink to the murky depths;
Lost in the sands of time,
Like so many loves before.

PretEND

                        I loved.
                    You pretended.
                      We ended.

Surface

No one is perfect;
We are all:
A little broken
A little scuffed
A little damaged.

Some are just better
At keeping it all
Under the surface.

Dissociation

How can you envisage
What you could become,
If you cannot even face
What you have done?

If you run from everything that is difficult, how do you think you can achieve anything worthwhile? You have to put in the hard yards to reap the rewards.

Strings

You control the strings –
You pull them here
You push them there;
You make them dance
You make them sing.
Believe you're in control.

Queen of the drama
You believe it's all about you
They are all of the pieces,
And that you are the glue.
Keep them all within your reach;
That you know what they must do.

Perhaps it's time to cut your ties
Let go and watch them fall.
For no matter how hard you try
Their life is out of your control.
Quickly, cut the strings, let them fly
Before they break free and run;
Leaving you to cry
Whilst you sit here all alone.

You cannot control the lives of others and the longer and tighter you hold the strings, the stronger they pull and the further they run.

Lantern

When you let another carry the lamp
And lead the way, your trust misplaced when
Living your life, their way
Leads you to a place
You do not wish to stay.

If you find yourself in a situation where you are unsure of the correct direction to take, asking the opinions of those around you can give you a general guide; however, only you know what is right for you in the end.

If you blindly follow someone's advice without thinking about the outcomes, you could find yourself in a situation you never wanted to be. Remain mindful when making decisions.

Bliss

If I could
Pull a ruse
To stun
And confuse,
Make my brain
Look the other way,
I would cut loose;
Run for a place –
An escape –
To where
My thoughts and emotions
Would be bemused.
That my friends,
Would be
Limitless bliss.

One of the interesting skills I discovered through meditation is the ability to get my mind to stop. It is always ticking away and there are times where I just don't have the energy to listen to the noise. I will then lay on the floor, close my eyes and allow my mind settle.

Infected

If you cover yourself
In your own poisonous filth,
You'll infect yourself, so you
Believe everything is as
You see and feel.

Sometimes you need to take a step out of the situation to understand what is really happening. It makes it difficult when you are within the moment to notice anything other than that moment.

How Can I?

The deck of life shuffled, the cards dealt face down.
Puzzled, I arrange them as best I can.
Hands fly, chips swirl; not going as I had planned.
Sit back, take a breath – this will all turn around.

How can I trust it will all work out and let it be
When the signs point to disappointment and misery?
How can I sit back and drift effortlessly
Let the world and life flow past without me?

The man to my left in his pinstriped suit
A cocky smile, false bravado; honesty on mute.
Declares, "I'm all in" and pushes forward his loot.
Another's hand of two pair renders his bluff moot.

How can I give myself when all has been taken
When I poured out my heart and its worth was mistaken.
How can I push forth in silence; no explanation
Let it fade into nothing with no information.

The woman sits poised so elegantly.
Her beauty radiates so effortlessly.
Plays each hand so quietly;
Her mystery encapsulates me so readily.

How can I fall for someone whose insides I cannot see?
Their beating heart, their armoured mind; a twisted mystery.
How can I explore them without being denied viciously?
The possibility damaged irreparably.

Final hand – left to the woman and me
Her bid enticing, the fear removed; I bid free.
Cards turned face up, my mind frozen in horror as I see
The woman walks away, with everything – except me.

How can I love again when my heart is broken?
Placed my belief in someone and was mistaken.
Kept on giving until all was taken;
To my very core I have been shaken.

Belief

If you believe
Everyone sees
The world in
Your way
Be prepared
For a life
Of misery
And disarray.

Pretend

Pretending to be
Someone you're not
Hurts everyone
When you stop.

If you spend all of your energy pretending to be something you're not, either to impress someone or to fit in with the crowd, you may find that it makes you feel uncomfortable. If you know you are not being your true self, then being something else is difficult; it takes a lot of time and energy to live a lie and be something you are not.

When you then decide to let go of the mask and show your true self, don't be surprised if people then reject you. Instead, have some integrity and strength and be who you truly are.

If you are uncomfortable with yourself, your life or particular situation, don't throw more energy at it; be honest with yourself and discover what is making you uncomfortable. Discover you and you won't be so tired from running away.

Hollow Halls

                Even though you're never mentioned
                You wander the haunted halls of my mind
                And the hollow holes you burnt in my heart.

Fragments

The ghosts of love
Lost long ago
Invade edges of your mind;
Odours lingering in the air
Stains upon the walls
The burnt dishes and pans
Lost socks lying on the floor.

Fragments left behind
To torture and leave you
In irreparable disrepair.

Hide

The pain of
Loving and losing
Would be nothing
Compared to
Pretending and excusing.

In our interactions with people (both yourself and others), are you yourself or are you trying to be someone else?

One thing I don't understand is how people say it takes years to get to know someone (in a romantic relationship sense). People try to say that "people change", when in reality they were pretending to be someone they THOUGHT they should be in order to get the other person to connect with them. Then as they become comfortable, they slowly show their true selves.

How about you put in your all from day one, be yourself, so when that person falls in love with you, they fall in love with the true you. I remember the first time I met my wife; we were eating lunch and talking when she made me laugh so hard I had my face covered.

That was when she poked me on the end of the nose. In that moment, I knew that she was weird and even though she didn't mean to let it out so soon, I knew that she felt comfortable around me to be herself.

Don't hide your true self, for you never know who is looking for you.

Slow

Is it speed you long for?
The quickest method to reach
Your next destination.
Find a seat on your own
So it's easier to ignore
The people, the signs;
Purely a distraction.

The city bleeds into the horizon,
Colours fade as the sun sets.
Yet, you keep your eyes blurred;
If you don't notice the change
You can't be disturbed by
The possibility that it will
All be gone. Forever.

If you are so caught up in your beliefs and refuse to listen to other points of view or acknowledge others' experiences, you can miss the opportunity to develop a more rounded view. You don't have to adopt their view, but if you understand where they are coming from, it will make it easier to feel compassion towards them.

Knowing

Knowing
When to do
something
To give
everything
Is just as
important as
Knowing
When to do
and say
Nothing.

Signals

The beauty of a painting
In the face of an angel;
The body of a goddess
Had my breath escaping.

But nevertheless,

There is no indication
To the softness of your soul.

Without an invitation,
I can only guess;
With little to no justification.

Don't judge what is invisible by what is visible.

If You'd Told Me (I Wouldn't Have Believed You)

If you'd told me just one year ago
That my whole world would change
I would've wondered how you knew
And were you sure it was true?

The people I know, the places I go
Deserted and stripped bare.
It has all become alien;
Must learn to live again.

If you'd told me –
I would have my heart torn out,
I would discover what my life is truly about,
I would become a writer and musician,
I would be in this new position,
I would travel the world,
I would uncover secrets waiting to be told –
I wouldn't have believed you.

If you'd told me just one year ago
That I'd find my true course
That I'd no longer be lost
I'd ask you – how so?

All these things hidden and unknown
That I was just waiting to be shown
Have to be patient; can't rush this, no.
In for the ride; let's see where this goes.

BARGAINING

My Own Man

Made the decision, the hard call.
To be here, by myself; do it on my own.
The phone doesn't beep, doesn't ring at all.
Got to be my own man; got to do this alone.

No one here in the evening, no one here at night.
No one here in the morning; their smile oh so bright.
No one here in the winter, to hold and snuggle tight.
No one here in the summer; but I know it'll be alright.

I need to find the answers, to discover the truth.
To uncover the feelings, the meaning of my true self.
Do it all here now, do it in my youth
Before it catches up with me, when I cannot be helped.

There's one thing I know dear, one thing that holds true
That deep gut feeling that it will all be renewed.
Even though I sit here alone – the past, it is through
Someday, somehow, it will all turn out and start anew.

Respect

Your wishes were vague
Open ended and confusing,
In the end – it was you I was losing.
Watching your lips moving, hearing nothing;
Internal heart destruction
Because of what was coming.

Lived in a daze, a state of delusion
Continued in the same way,
Believing all would be okay.
One look in your eyes – cold with exclusion;
What went wrong, what had (or hadn't) I done?
Sadness and disbelief did reign.

Years have passed, emotion bled through.
Many things I have done; all but some,
Because of my love for you.
No drunken calls at 1 a.m.,
Wishing, pleading for "us" to be again.
No spontaneous visits to catch you off guard.
No standing in the shadows; watching from afar.

I respect your journey, truly, I do.
Sometimes I wish I could do the same;
Sell everything I own and run away too.
But right now, it's not the answer,
Right here I'll stay
Hope you find your answers, tell me about it one day.
...
....
......

Time has passed.
Many things have changed.
But through it all, there are some that remain.

And maybe,

Just maybe…

You'll discover the same.

Fair Trade

You traded a heart of gold
For hearts of coal
That will leave you dirty
And your soul
Empty and cold.

Choices & Losses

Take pity on the fool –
A life laid out on
A silver platter;
Chose to throw
it all away,
To take their chance
in life's lottery pool.

Take pity on the fool –
When they lose everything
They could ever want;
Could ever need.
Lost and cast astray;
A hole burning deep
Within their soul.

Snake Eyes

Roll the dice to try your luck.

A pair of snake eyes
Have taken all you have,
Instead of doubling
More than enough.

Greed and envy will take all you have, until you're left with nothing.

Hold

When you let go of the good
To take hold of the bad
Eventually, one day
You'll miss everything you had.

Waiting

I can't remember what was the trigger
That forced my lungs to wheeze
Pushed me into a bent over figure
As I continued to cough, splutter and sneeze.

When I straightened and looked down
The tissue was speckled with blood
My brow turned to a frown
My eyes began to flood.

Where had this come from?
Why hadn't I noticed before?
Had it been going on for long?
The answers to these questions – unsure.

I saw all the specialists
Consulted with the best
They assured me it wouldn't be missed
But I had to take the test.

I begged and I reasoned
Surely this couldn't be true?
There had to be an explanation
This life couldn't be through.

The minutes, hours and days ticked by
A continuous struggle– ropes around my chest
I thought I was going to die
Couldn't imagine what came next.

My mind was spinning, I couldn't focus
Filled with thoughts of losing it all
Everything changed with little notice
Sitting in silence, waiting for the hammer to fall.

Ladder of Love

Read from the last line upwards.

So far down I don't hear you hit the ground.
Disappear between the clouds
Watch you fall from up high
I see you fingers slip
Our love wasn't made to last.
But it wasn't destined to be;
I ask you to remain steadfast.
You ask me to let go, to let you fall
My strength is just not enough.
I ask you questions and listen intently.
Talk softly, caress gently
Shelter you from the gusts
Spread my feet wide
I stand by your side
Your resolve carried away by the wind.
The rungs too high, the air too thin
That we'll make it, mighty we will stand.
I say not to let go of my hand
Your feet begin to drag
Soon I see your arms droop
Before you tire us to death.
I ask you to rest, take a breath
The weary eyes; brow furrowed in concern.
I look at your face and discern
High enough to see other lands.
Halfway up, pulling me by the hand
Your arms will be there to pull you through.
That if your legs grow weak
You scoff, you know what to do
Or you may lose your way.
Don't rush, don't push
One rung at a time they all say
Do whatever it takes.
Determined to make it
Your lips part and a sigh escapes
Only visible from great heights.
The delicate landscapes
Dazzled by the shining lights
Engulf and ignite your lungs.
Let the sweet, intoxicating smell
Take in a deep breath
Rung by rung
Climbing the ladder of love

Light of Hindsight

Wouldn't we wish
To hear the words escape from their lips;
To be shown everything that we had missed?

Unfortunately, hindsight is bliss.

If Only

If only...
The thought will leave you
Cold, confused
Frustrated and blue;
Your mind it will abuse.
Until it leaves you lonely.

If Only...something I hear from many people is that they wish they could do something, but <insert excuse here>. This will eventually turn into "if only I had done..." as if it justifies their choice.

However, this doesn't make sense for a couple of reasons:
1. If you really wanted to, you would have.
2. You'll keep thinking about it until you do.

Why not give it a go? Don't sit and let your mind pull you down with negativity – put in the work and focus on the outcome. Your mind will tell you a lot of stories, but you can choose which to believe.

Lonely Goals

Whilst working towards
Your goals you wish to achieve
Doing them alone
May not be what you need.

Something that I see many articles written about is the attitude that everyone should be single in their 20s; running around and living up life, travelling, partying and basically ignoring responsibly all while "finding yourself". Somehow saying that you can start thinking about being a responsible person when you hit thirty; as if it's some sort of magical cure for selfishness and stupidity.

What would be better said is the idea that they should be looking at themselves and discovering what their values are. Determining what their passions are and how they want to interact with others and the world around them.

Life cannot be written as a "one size fits all" journey. Perhaps you will find someone that loves you and it is in conflict with your personal goals. Working to accommodate them instead of turning your back because someone else said so, is a more fulfilling experience; you'll have someone to share your loss and success with.

Oh Well, What If

I'd rather look back
On my life and say:
"Oh well"
Instead of:
"What if"

This is why I always give 110%. Yes, a clichéd saying, but passion is one of the big three drivers in my life. Being dedicated and always doing your best, caring about your actions and how they affect others are things that will help you to grow as a person.

Reborn

Exiled from my home
Rocks thrown at me from the door;
I disappeared to distant lands.
I swam across the iciest seas
I climbed the tallest mountains
I stumbled the widest desert sands
I slayed the largest demons.
I return a reborn man.

Trembling, I extend my hand
To knock on the closed door.

Realisation

I just realised
That my world
Is still spinning;
With or without you.

Tangled

The path we were on was clear;
No troubles to be had, no obstacles in our way.
The call of the jungle was strong;
You let go of my hand and ran away.

Deep under the canopy you did run,
I stood my ground, waited for your return.
But with the setting of the sun
My heart fill with grave concern.

My head dropped, away I did turn;
I had stood in place for far too long.
Time for me to accept you're gone
Before my skin begins to burn.

Imagining what you've seen,
Wondering if it's as good as it seemed.
Is the sky as blue? Is the grass as green?
Air grows thicker, horizon shimmers;
Perhaps it was only a glimmer.

Deeper and deeper you did go
Trees growing closer
Canopy so thick, no longer see the sky
The right way to turn, no longer did you know.

Snakes slither across your path,
In pursuit of their next victim;
Coiling around your calves
To pull you down with them.

Caimans watching from afar,
Eyes dart back and forth –
Following your every move.
Lying in wait for a single mistake;
One bite and you're through.

You hunger, you thirst
Feet are weary; eyes ready to burst.
The berries seem delicious; succulent and sweet.
But beware; eat them if you dare.

Exhausted, you rest your crown,
As the fog rolls in and covers the ground.
As night falls, snakes dangle down;
I hope you don't rise to find yourself tangled.

ANGER

Perfection

You wanted perfection
So you walked away from
A soul to soul connection.

No one in this world is perfect; we all have our flaws and shortcomings. Before you allow the negative thoughts to ruin a relationship, stop and think about the following: do they care for you? Do you feel safe in their presence? Can you talk to them about anything? Do you sleep better next to them? Stop and look at the positive.

Don't destroy what you have for the possibility of perfection – it's unrealistic.

Trojan

A Trojan let loose
Upon those within your noose.
Silent and invisible you sneak,
Your true intentions hidden,
Remain unaware of your
Deception and deceit.

Climbing cowardly through
The web, espionage and blackmail
To keep you ahead;
Aboard the money train
Without merit or claim,
Do what it take to escape.

Hide in the shadows
Spread spam and lies
To evade the sorrow.
When finally captured,
You'll beg and plead
For release.

There are a lot of fake people in this world; some of those will say things about you behind your back, while others will lie straight to your face. Learning to pick a chameleon in the crowd is a tough ask, but once you notice, make sure you stay out of their grasp.

Mask

You have faces that no one else sees.
How can anyone ever truly believe?

What Counts

What it seems to be
May not be what it
Needs to be;
What needs to be,
Is the way it
Has always been.

It's easy for someone to change the appearance of themselves or their lives to impress others.

However, when they remove their mask, what is really underneath? What was it that they felt they had to hide?

Savage

Men and women
Who are raised
By wolves will
Become savages.

Be careful whom you let into your life, for their past may become your future.

No Better

When you believe
You are better
Than another,
You become
No better
Than any other.

Deceive

You let me believe
There was more to see,
To put my heart
In you and breathe.

You let me believe
That you'd love me
Forever more.
Through it all,
I held on;
Never let you go.

You even smiled
As you let go,
Turned off the light
And closed the door.

White Lie

"I Love You" she said…
What harm could a little white lie do?

It took my ability to trust
Gripped in the hold of fear
Squeezed it into dust.
It closed my heart's doors
Chained and covered in moss;
No one comes knocking anymore.
It put my past on looping replay
A black and white horror
The running feature, every single day.

It destroyed me; through and through.

Spilt

"It's not like someone died"
You said while plunging
The knife between my ribs.

As you walked out the door
I slumped forward –
My love
My dreams
My heart
Spilling out onto the floor.

Gone

I gave you my everything.
I gave you my all.
And if I could have,
I would have given more.

But you didn't appreciate.
Not one bit; no, not at all.
Took. Took again; then
Took some more.
Until everything
I ever had was gone.

Promises

Girls and boys lie
Whilst the
Men and women cry.

One Day

"Maybe one day…"
Is what you said.

Maybe one day
You'll become
A decent person
instead.

Thanks to You

Thanks to you
There were pieces of my heart and soul
Scattered about the floor;
Years of my love dashed and destroyed
When you walked out the door.
Replaced with tears, pain and anguish
Sleepless nights and endless days;
Prayed for your return to extinguish
The raging flames that consumed my mind;
Imagined all the things I could do,
Everything I could say.

Thanks to you
I ambled aimlessly, every single day;
Nothing could hold me in happiness,
At a moment's notice, it would replay.
Sat in silence, asked on repeat –
Why?
Tried to sift truth from lies;
The longer I tried, I began to realise
It was all a waste of time.
Insecurity and immaturity
The only things left to find.

Thanks to you
I tested the water of life,
Found the fire that helped me thrive.
Tore away life's lies, escaped the net of doubt
So that I may be proud.
Unlocked hidden rooms,
The emptiness began to fill;
The fog is lifting, I can see through the gloom.

I know you'll be back one day,
However, there's nothing left for you here;
Not a word left to say.
For you are the coward, led by fear
Taken down a soggy, beaten path
Where many have trod; their ruins remain.
I won't be there to save you; I will refrain
Good luck on your journey
You're going to need it one day.

Changed

Oh, if only you knew
The pain you put me through.
Forever, I have been changed;
I'll never, ever be the same.

Personal Format

C:\Users\ME> CD..
C:\Users> CD..
C:\> Deltree C:\Memories
ERROR: DIRECTORY CORRUPTED. CANNOT BE DELETED.

C:\> FORMAT C:
WARNING! ALL DATA ON NON-REMOVABLE DISK DRIVE C:
WILL BE LOST.
PROCEED WITH FORMAT (Y/N)? Y

I'd rather format my mind
Than leave fragments
Of you behind.

Letter

To the girl who broke my heart,

Could you please return
The pieces of me you stole
So that I can give them to someone
Who deserves to be loved
Completely and unconditionally?

If you're not going to use them
I want to give it to someone
Who will cherish my love
Not abuse and discard
When they decide
They've had enough.

Your understanding and cooperation
Would be greatly appreciated;
But I highly doubt you have neither
The integrity nor the regard or concern
To do what is right; to show honour.
From your actions, that much I can discern.

Regards,

The man who's broken because you destroyed the boy's ability to believe.

Repackaged

Time we spent – wasted.
Places we went – eroded.
Memories we made – erased.
Friends we had – disowned.
Promises you made – disbelieved.
Lies you told – forgotten.
Love you stole – returned.
Pain you caused – healed.

The boy I was – gone.
The man I am – here.
The love inside – repackaged.

It

When you had it –
You didn't want it.
When you rejected it –
You broke it.
When you ignored it –
You killed it.

But when you want it –
You can't have it.
When you plead for it –
You can't have it.
When you beg for it –
You can't have it.

For it
Now belongs
To someone else.

Commitment

I know many explicit words.
The longest and most
offensive?

Commitment.

It seems that the subject of commitment is a taboo subject in today's society. It seems no one want to stick at anything anymore, claiming "it's too hard!", "there's plenty more fish in the sea", "I can't be bothered". A generation of people that have a sense of entitlement; believing that they should have everything now and if they don't, they should complain about it. However, are they putting in the hard work? The time, the energy and the love to gain (and maintain) the things they long for?

Life's a bitch and then you die. You can either accept that nothing and no one is perfect and that you have to put in the effort or you can search for shortcuts. However, what you put in, is what you get back, so if you put in a half arsed effort, expect a half arsed result.

If something or someone means something to you, don't give up. Always work at it. It may not work out, but at least you gave it your everything and that's all anyone can ask for.

Bittersweet

The bitter truth
Tastes better than
A sweet lie.

In situations where you have the opportunity to sugar coat a situation to save someone's feelings; here's a tip – don't. It hurts so much more when the truth comes out and your integrity is compromised, if not destroyed.

What Goes Around

> The boomerang of karma –
> A dangerous tool.
> Throw it nicely
> And it shall return
> Back to you.
> Throw it with malice
> And it may take
> Days. Weeks.
> Years. Decades.
>
> But eventually
> It will return
> Silent and deadly
> To cause damage
> and fractures;
> The scars of which
> May never fade.

I find karma interesting; I'm not the person that believes in spiritual things, but I do believe in kindness and compassion. I feel that if you intentionally, knowingly or willingly treat someone poorly, in a way that demeans them, makes them feel physical, emotional or mental pain or deliberately make fun of their weaknesses, instead of helping them, karma is coming for you. It doesn't matter how long, but eventually, it will catch you.

You may be on the lookout for it, scoff at it or feel invincible, but the truth is, karma never forgets. It will hunt you down and take you out.

Remain humble.

Heartbreak's Masterpiece

I am just
One of
Heartbreak's
Many masterpieces.

There are two sayings which are applicable here: "what doesn't kill you, makes you stronger" and "It can either destroy, define or drive you. You choose."

I remember when I was in the midst of the pain, it felt as if it was all encompassing and that there would never be an escape. In that moment, I was at my lowest point and I was choosing between life and death – to give up, no longer care and end everything. That was the destroy part.

I also remember being able to discuss my pain; recite it like a poem and express it to those that would care to listen. I would use the pain as a shield and as a character blurb. That was the define part.

However, what I discovered was the reason the pain existed was caused by my dislike for people that showed a lack of honesty, respect, empathy, authenticity and integrity. That is what drives me now; my desire to help people to help themselves and create understanding and compassion between people.

So, what do you choose?

DEPRESSION

Tears

As she cried, little did she know he was crying too.
Not silent, pitiful tears, but deep guttural cries.

Tears so voluminous they drowned his lashes,
Spilling into his mouth and soaking his skin.
Tears so thick they stopped his breath,
Made his chest heave with each laboured gasp.
Tears so heavy they made him collapse to his knees,
Pinning him painfully in place.
Tears so dark they blanketed the sky,
Swallowing his soul.
Tears so tiring they stole his sleep,
Making him weak.

Little did she know, he cried too.

Wake

Laugh so loud

Smile so wide

Hug so tight

Kiss so gently

Love so tenderly

Care so much

Feel so whole.

WAKE

Cry so loud

Hole so wide

Chest so tight

Tremble so gently

Whisper so tenderly

Miss so much

Feel so alone.

Sometimes, it's better to stay asleep.

How Do You

How do you
Close the door
On the one
That was there
Each time you called?

How do you
Run so far
Disappear from him
Pretend as if
You never existed at all?

How do you
Lay your head
Down each night
Without a thought
Of what you did?

How do you
Continue your life
Without a word
Not even sorry
Show remorse, heaven forbid.

So, how do you?

False Hope

False hope
Is where
Dreams and lives
Go to die.

False hope causes people to continually pour their energy and beliefs into pointless endeavours until they have nothing left.

All's Fair

Lies as your ammunition
Emotions as your soldiers
Shame as your bunker
Deceit as your tactics
Friends as your confidantes
Promises as your propaganda.

When you turned and declared war
Pitted my heart against yours
One of flesh against one of steel
For ceasefire, I appealed;
My soul peppered with bullets.

Dreams spilt as tears fell
Love burnt to the ground;
My mind barren and desolate
Broken and tormented.
I closed my eyes
And welcomed the end.

Life and Death

In trying to save me
You killed me.

Loneliness

The ice cold darkness
Rolls in once more
But there's no one here
To keep me warm.

All the love and happiness
Have disappeared and gone;
Refrain from reaching out,
Must stay strong.

Days, nights, they smash into one.
No one to turn to; nowhere to run.
Eternal loneliness my only friend;
Knowing I'm finished; this is my end.

How did it turn out like this?
What signs did I miss?
Trying to understand, sitting here alone,
Wishing this all could be undone.
Can't replay the past
Once it slips from your grasp.

Drag myself to my feet,
Stagger forth, step by step.
I hope I may meet
Someone that can accept
Me for me, including all
Of the faults that lie between;
Someone who brings out my best.

One day, the loneliness will be gone
Forget all the pain; chains on my heart torn.
But until that day comes
Loneliness will reign number one.

Wounds

All that's left of us
Are the wounds.

Experiences may define you, but don't let them confine you.

Cell

I see you enter this cell
Of your own design and detail
Watch as you turn the key
Set infinity as your bail.
Watch as you lock yourself
Into your own personal hell.

I scream. I plead. I coax.
I extend my hand; I reach out
Explain it's you I love most.

Please, pass me the key
Let me help you
Set yourself free.
For when you go into lockdown
The darkness
Will make love hard to see.

Burnt

You injected venom
Deep in my heart and mind.
With the passing of time
Into my soul it did bleed.

Mixed with my blood,
Cause my tears to flood.
As I lost all sense of me;
Of the man I am meant to be.

Muscles seize, frozen in place,
My mind became my prison;
No bars, no doors, no locks,
Yet I cannot escape.

Time continues to pass,
I know this cannot last;
These scars have begun healing –
Wounds now only slowly bleeding.

Aftermath

Eyes pressed tightly shut as I wait
For the dust to settle and the echoing screams to stop.
I stumble to my feet and examine the ruins
Of shattered dreams and fallen mountain tops.

I turned on the spot – hearts and souls
Laying slaughtered on the ground,
Throats gurgling and low moans
The only sounds.

I search for survivors,
Armed with only my knife
Going from door to door
Seeking signs of life.

Hands twitch, breathing shallow
Each careful footstep echoes.
Waiting for a single soul
To try to steal my own.

I scan the horizon in fear.
A repeat of the past;
the pain and anguish come to stay.
Old demons resurrected,
Once again I will have to slay.
Nightmares reborn;
Crushing memories on display.

Once I was a Man who stood his ground;
Dependable, stable and committed –
Never let the one he loved down.
Now I am a boy who is scared to stay and stick around
Afraid to be vulnerable and open; easier to leave town.

I now stumble my way along this twisting path
The remnants of my soul to guide me in the aftermath.

Depth

Slumped at the bottom of the well,
Looking up at the small speck
Of light glistening above.
Shivering, core so cold,
Been living here too long;
No energy to climb jagged footholds.
Slime on the walls, rats at your feet,
Scream until your lungs are raw;
No one hears your desperate call
As your loneliness echoes on.

The stones haphazard, digging in your back.
The months roll by; of time you've lost track.
Surrounded by the skeletons
Of all that have perished.
This life cannot be accepted;
Push your back against the wall
Pull yourself from this hell,
Return to all you love and cherish.

Depression is a personal hell which only you can escape. It may feel like there is no way out, but by remaining present, practising mindfulness and being positive (knowing that bad things don't last forever) – your outlook on life will change, and as a result, things will become easier.

There may be dark days in which you may wish to give up and remain at the bottom of your well, where no one can hurt you; but if you stay there you will rot and life will evade you.

Star

Frozen in horror as I
Witness my destruction;
The breaking of my heart,
The shattering of my soul.

Pick up my pieces and
Turn them in my hands,
Collect the most beautiful;
To be used in other plans.

Clearing the path of debris
Make a space for something new,
New names, new faces,
In undiscovered places.

Raise my eyes to
The shimmering light.
Take a step forward,
Before I begin to run;
I could tell that everything
Would be alright.

Abstruse

Anxiety,

Your atrociously abstruse attacks appal me.

Sincerely,
All.

I am a bit of a worrier. I worry about my relationship falling apart, I worry about not being financially stable, I worry about the state of the planet and the crazy things that go on. Some of these I can have an effect upon, but many I cannot.

I know what it's like to have anxiety that cripples you to the point where you cannot move, make a decision, sleep or even breathe. It's at times like this that being able to make space for the feelings and allow them to pass is important. Also, do not be ashamed of the feelings; almost everyone has experienced them at some point in their life and if they are negatively impacting on your life, speaking out and getting help can make a world of difference. Asking for help does not make you weak.

Curse

I'm teetering on the edge –
Worried the world will destruct
Our hands hovering above the button.
Worried my love will walk away
Into the arms of another.
Worried that those around
Will try to cut me down.
Worried I will lose all I have
It will become what I had.

Anxiety: a curse
That won't let you breathe;
Can never feel quite at ease.
Living in the moment –
In your world you must immerse.

Practising mindfulness is very useful at times when the waves try to roll over you.

Feel

I feel the tears just behind my eyes
I feel the tightness in my chest
I feel the tingle in my nose
I feel the air ruffling in my hair
I feel the words penetrate my brain
I feel the blanket of sorrow on my soul.

Regardless of it all
I won't let it hold me down
Be the very best I can be
Until joy is all that I feel.

Overthinking

The greatest gift for any writer is

        OVERTHINKING

            is the cruellest curse for anyone.

One thing that writers do (well at least I do) is think. A lot. This allows pieces of writing to formulate in my mind; what the message is and how to phrase it.

Unfortunately, it is also a curse. Overthinking leads to worry (anxiety) which can lead to sadness, which could even lead to depression; all with just thoughts!

The mind is a powerful tool – either constructive or destructive, depending on what it's telling you and what you choose to hear and believe – practising mindfulness is crucial; being aware of what you think and feel is important and being able to separate the useful from the trash is just as important.

Don't believe everything you think.

Present

Everything before now
Is long gone
Everything after today
Does not exist
Yet I feel as if
I'm losing all I have;
The only one I need.

Pain

>   It
>   still
>   hurts.

For all the people that have been hurt in one way or another, healing takes a long time and it is okay. Don't believe that you are weak just because people say that you should be over it and don't be afraid to say that you're not okay.

Bottling up and avoiding your thoughts and emotions only causes more negativity. Embrace who you are; your scars and all, for those are what make you beautiful.

ACCEPTANCE

Therapy

I have the memories in my head
I have the scars across my heart.
I pick up this pen –
Let the therapy start.

Forgive

Forgive.
Forget.
Focus on fulfilment.

Abscess

Active avoidance
Is the Achilles heel
Of healing.

If you have pain that you run from and avoid dealing with it, eventually it can kill you.

Pain – physical or mental – tells you of something that's amiss. Ignore it at your own peril.

Scar Tissue

I strip down, standing naked in front of the mirror. I examine my wounds, the remains of years past. Of the hearts that I've held, the laughter I've shared; each one a lesson, a unique experience. Some spanned what seemed to be eons, others, only an instant; all of them uncovering a piece of me I had never seen before.

The wounds are old, pink and white, deep scars covered; a veil pulled thin, hiding the pain that lurks deep within. Time taken out to rest and recover, to unravel the secrets I'm meant to discover.

I've been beaten, thrashed to within an inch of my life.
I've been cut open, bled profusely upon the floor.
I've been poisoned, choking whilst crawling to the door.
I've been run down, organs rupture whilst clutching my chest.
I've been choked slowly, hands tightening round my neck.
I've been drowned, washed ashore; nowhere to be found.

But I'm still alive.

I'll never stop living.
I'll always give my best.
I'll never stop learning.
I'll rise above it all;
I'll conquer this pain
Residing in my soul.

Knight

I don't want to be the knight in shining armour
Riding in to save the day.
For I am the man with scars and flaws;
With arms wide open, all of them on display.

Even though my suit is speckled
With spots of rust and decay,
You love me still and
You choose to stay.

Behind These Eyes

There's more to me
Much more to see
Behind these eyes;
So many tears
They have cried.

Everyone has their own story; the depths of which we rarely get to see. However, everything they have been through up to this point has brought them to exactly this point in time. How can you judge their actions if you don't know their history? If you had walked their path, would you have done the same?

Exploding Passion

Pulled the pin
Threw the grenade.
Lobbing it into my heart.
It exploded;
Sending shards of love
Whizzing through my body,
my organs they bombard.
Instead of killing me
Making me bleed from within,
They ignite my everything –
Something interesting
Is about to begin.

The passion I held
Once only for one
Now spread throughout;
It touches anything
That I dare care about.

I give my everything
Always do my best;
Because in the end
That's all I can accept.

Sometimes, the things that seem the worst, turn out to be the best.

Surrender

Hold our memories so close,
They provide no guidance, feeling lost;
No idea, no direction, no signs on the post.
The one I wanted most –
I had to surrender.

My heart said yes, my head said no
Undecided, someone show me the way to go.
No longer can I live this way,
Looking forward to a sweet escape –
I had to surrender.

I wrote it out, let the feelings free
Locked it out, sent it away forever.
No longer inside, no longer a part of me
Feeling free, feeling lighter, feeling better –
I had to surrender.

Open up my mind, bear my soul
Unchain my heart; allow someone to hold.
Take it slow, play it safe
Time to be had, this isn't a race.

But first I had to let go,
So glad I was able to surrender.

Believe

Another day I wake up cold and alone
Roll over reaching out; no one there to hold.
My heart sinks, reality bleeds back in.

I must believe it, know that it's true;
No reason why, there aren't any signs,
That all will be okay, that it's not too late.
I must believe it, trust and not stipulate.

Living my own life now everyone is gone
Doing exactly what I need, what I must
To discover the real me,
The man hidden below.

No signs on this path to show the way,
Must trust in myself that I'll make it anyway.
No need for a shoulder, I still have my feet,
Carry me to victory from the clutches of defeat.

This all seems crazy
So amazingly unreal,
Cast adrift in the world
No one's hand to hold.
Bruised and battered
By the twists and the turns,
But each day I grow stronger,
Until normality returns.

Open Eyes

As I looked into
the mirror
I realised I had
said goodbye
To my old reality,
my old self
And welcomed
the new
With open eyes.

Sanity

As much as it makes your heart break
You cannot save everyone;
For your own sanity's sake.

True You

Are you so afraid of yourself
That you'd rather leave your soul
Collecting dust; just sitting on a shelf
Whilst you pretend to be someone else?

Why pretend to be someone else? To copy? To fit in? You are unique and that is why you are interesting. Look inside to discover yourself instead of comparing with everyone else.

Weird

Don't change you weird
Embrace your weird.

What makes you, you? If someone asked you to describe yourself in a sentence, what would you say?

Everyone is different, no matter how similar they may seem. The things that make you different – your strengths, your likes, your habits, your sayings, your favourite music or food and the flip side – your weaknesses, your faults, your frustrations and your dislikes…these are the things that make you unique.

Embrace your differences and work on your shortcomings, but always value yourself. Why be someone else when you can only be you?

Be True

                Be True.
                Be only you.

Only you, can be you.

Better

Don't be bitter
Because
Someone is better.

There will always be someone out there who is "better" – better at sport, music, art, has more money or possessions or is more attractive – it's a fact. You could sit there and get upset that they have it "better" than you or you could congratulate them on their successes and use it as motivation to work at your own ambitions to become the best version of yourself.

Guide

You can't make people
Believe what you know;
You can only guide the way
And let them discover it
On their own.

When someone is so set in their beliefs and ways that they can't see any other – regardless of the impact it is having on them or others around them – the only thing you can do is be patient and lead the way by example.

Incarcerated

A man who was free, open and alive –
In love, a happy man; no struggles to survive.
Until his world was torn, mind now encased
In concrete and steel; happiness now replaced
With confusion, fear and sadness.
A mind full of colour now bleeds darkness.

Each day a repeat, thoughts replayed
Sapping his strength; motivation frayed.
Whispers in the shadows fills him with lies,
Unable to see reality, what was before his eyes.

No need to engage with the world,
Comfort found in the wine he swirled.
Continues to refill the glass –
An easy way to stay incarcerated
In the prison of the past.

Steel bars cold against his cheeks,
Lukewarm compared to the tears he weeps.
Nightmares day and night, no release.
His heart and soul grow weak.

His mind is his dungeon,
Confusion the chains upon his feet.
The pain and sadness drag him
To the demise he will meet.

A new day brings no change,
No avenue for his escape;
To make a fresh start.
To depart would be his release,
Spring free from emotional prison;
The pulsing pain of a broken heart.

Hang from the ceiling, or
Land on jagged rocks;
Whatever it takes to silence
The relentless ticking of the clock.

There must be a way
To allow him to stay,
Connect with the world,
With those that cared;
Regardless of the pain.

Grief and Growth

If only he knew
How to explain
The thoughts and questions
That consumed his brain;
Made him question
If he would find happiness again.

He sat on the floor,
Took time out to renew
His back stretched out on the floor
His mind grew quiet
As the hope inside him grew.
Eyes opened and upon his return,
A gift uncovered, one he hadn't discerned.

Rose to his feet and grasped the handle,
To find the weakest spot, must light more candles.
Began to dig in the soil floor,
As all the exits were blocked –
Had to create his own door.

Dug day and night, each day he grew closer
To the happiness and freedom
He desperately longed for.
Never did his shovel swing slower,
Even when he struck rock or
Was showered in rancid water.
Resolve stayed strong,
His motivation never faltered.

Dug for months it seemed
In pitch blackness;
No candles remain to guide his travels;
No need for exactness.
The passage turned and twisted,
It ran for miles.
His cell no longer existed,
All he could do was smile.

His arms now weak, back is strained
As he struck the final blow;
In sunshine and sweet relief he was rained.
The path nowhere near complete, but
No longer against those voices
Would he have to compete.
For now, the incarceration was over,
Time to live his life again.

Suitcase

I have travelled
From place to place
On my journey
Upon Earth's face.
Carrying with me
A deep suitcase
Where memories
Thoughts and emotions
I have placed.
Some are wonderful
Lovely and happy;
Whilst others are sad
Or traumatic and
send me batty.

The longer I travel
The heavier it becomes
'til I can no longer move;
Its weight a few tonne.

As I sat and I rested
As tears fell from my eyes,
I discovered an answer;
Values I could live by.

See, I understood
That they are not real –
Those demons in the case –
Only things I can feel.
As soon as I let them escape
I would begin to heal.
I dropped the case
On the side of the road
Enter my new life
Without their crippling load.

When you fuse with your thoughts and emotions as real entities, happening here and now, they can quite easily freeze you in place. If you let them be and let them travel past you, life becomes easier.

It's Time

It's time to blow out the candles
It's time to let things go.
It's time to raise the curtain
It's time to go on with the show.

It's time to tie loose ends
It's time to clear the path.
It's time to live in full colour
It's time to endure life's wrath.

It's time to unlock doors
It's time to use my voice.
It's time to clear the cobwebs
It's time to make a choice.
It's time to find the truth
It's time to let colours shine.
It's time to speak one's mind
It's time to put life on the line.

It's time to live with no regrets
It's time to face the fear.
It's time to accept – come what may
It's time to dry the tears.

If you find yourself stuck in life or a particular situation, sometimes a bit of time allows things to become clear. But if after that time, you are still confused, perhaps you need to take a stand and do some hard work – something that most won't do – to find your way.

It may not be easy and you may risk a lot but in the end what is meant to happen will happen; at least this way you know you've done your all.

GROWTH

LEARN

For The Better

The worst
Give birth
To the best.

Sometimes, when it seems it couldn't get any worse, that is when you find something. Something that makes you, you. Something that makes you believe. Something that inspires you. Something that lifts you out of the darkened hole of self-pity and pain and makes the sun shine again.

Even though it may not seem like it right now, don't give up. Keep working, keep trying, keep living. For you never know what could be around the corner.

20/20

When someone
You love leaves
They take with them
The blindfold that
Allows you to
Truly see.

Badge of Honour

I don't carry this wound
As a badge of honour,
Nor do I try to bury it deep
Under lies and self-deceit.

Appropriate healing to ease the feeling;
To transform what makes my heart burn.
Meanwhile, the wound will remain,
Until it's ready to gradually fade away.

Demons

The more I write
The less I fight
With my demons
During the night.

Perspective

> If you look at life in a different light
> It may improve your sight.

By changing your perspective, you may notice something you never have before.

Learn to Love

> Learning
> To love
> Yourself
> Is harder than
> Choosing
> To love
> Someone else.

Choosing to love someone is easier than loving yourself because there is always the option of leaving, whereas you cannot leave yourself. You are stuck with all your imperfections, all of your flaws, all your weaknesses. No matter where you go, they will be right there with you. You can run as long and far as you like, you can hide on the darkest corner but they will always find you.

Do you hate yourself? Do you feel inadequate? Do you think you do not deserve what you have? These thoughts are all in your mind and as long as you listen to them, they will have control over you. Learning to accept who you are and to not compare yourself with others is the biggest step in the pursuit of happiness that you can take.

Avoid the negativity, ignore the hatred and build upon yourself; grow your character. Be your own inspiration.

Negative vs Positive

Negativity comes naturally;
Positivity takes
Practise and patience.

After going through a life change, I noticed how the world is inherently negative. Becoming more positive is useful, however, extremely unrealistic. Instead, by being realistic and understanding the things you can change and influence and those you cannot, life becomes easier.

Bounds

In this
Soulless society,
Selfishness
Knows no bounds.

People will do what they want, when they want. They will use you to further themselves, just because. Learn to spot them before they break you.

Change

People don't change,
Their masks
Just fall away.

Something I've learnt (which I'm sure many others have) is that people cannot readily change their habits.

Many people try to say that people change over time, and to some extent, this is true. However, in many instances, it's just that the person stops pretending to be someone they think they should be and begin living for themselves.

Being your authentic self is something that many people are afraid to do, in fear of offending others or not being liked and accepted. However, will you like yourself for trying to please everyone else?

Control

Live life in the present.
You can record memories,
But time is always moving forward.

You cannot pause in a moment.
You cannot rewind your life and
You can never, ever stop.

Appreciate

Appreciate
What you have
Before it becomes
What you had.

Don't get caught looking for more, wanting something else; for when you realise you want what you have, it may be gone.

Live and Learn

All people make mistakes.
Most people repeat them.
Many people learn from them.
Some people admit them.
Few people rectify them.

Which one are you?

Actions

Do things that:
Manage your mind
Build your body
Soothe your soul.

When you think about the things you do and the choices you make, do they contribute to your overall well-being? I feel happiest when I work on my fitness, mental state of mind and my soul.

I know that I neglect certain aspects at times, for example, my relationships with others. It may seem selfish, but it is because I need to focus on my own health before that of others.

What about your actions? Are you mindful of what you do and how it affects you and others?

Blind Truth

No two stories
Are ever the same:
Don't blindly believe
The truths they claim.

People around you may want to help you by giving you advice. This advice will most likely be based upon their experiences, and unfortunately, it may not be the best advice. Take their words with a sense of wonder and explore them, but do not accept them as gospel. What may have worked for them, may not work for you. They may also be jealous, envious or perhaps afraid that you will change and will deliberately try to sabotage you.

Escape your environment and learn more to gain a greater understanding.

Sleuth

Don't blindly accept
The words of others;
For their versions of events
Have a personal pretence
That changes the colour;
Which skews the scent.

Become an
Inquisitive sleuth
Discover for yourself
The actual truth.

For any issue in your life where you are unsure or need to understand, you may ask those around you for opinions or you may even try to work it out for yourself by thinking about it logically. Unfortunately, everyone (even your own mind!) has different takes on the situation and will all tell you something slightly different; they may even have their own personal agenda that changes what they share or say.

If you want to discover the truth, go to the source, ask the hard questions; go that extra mile. You may be surprised at what you find.

Changing Beauty

> Changing your outer beauty
> takes money.
> Changing your inner beauty
> takes time.
> Changing your core beauty
> takes focus.

Changing your outer appearance is easy – go to the gym, change your hair, put on makeup, put on a façade. You can control how others see your outer self; it is done by everyone on a daily basis to "fit in" with social norms. There are people whom you will click with instantly, but there will also be people that require more work to find a common ground, and this is where compromise is required to share a common view.

Changing how you think about the external environment takes time – if you want to be more responsive and accepting of the experiences and people around you, finding the positives in any situation takes time. Life is not without moments of joy, mediocrity and sorrow, but it's your attitude towards those moments which determine how you react to them.

Being consciously aware of how you think about yourself and the way you interact with others is not something that comes with ease. Understanding your demeanour requires you to take an outward perspective; which is a critical view (but not in destructive way) of your person and then taking action on those things which you feel are not productive for your happiness.

When your core beauty emanates through your inner and outer beauty so that people can see, believe and trust what you are like on the inside, is when you no longer have to protect the person within.

Boys to Men

Boys don't
become men;
Just as age doesn't
define character.

I've seen a plethora of articles on "real men", "how to know he's the one" or "signs he's a gentleman". The one thing that it always seems to come down to is respect.

It seems society is so caught up in trying to outshine one another that values such as kindness, integrity, honesty and commitment have been thrown out the window as if they are some kind of infectious garbage.

Instead, we are left with greedy (for money and power), self-gratifying, pleasure seeking individuals, all trying to "one up" each other, in order to be better than everyone else. How is that useful? Yes, giving your everything to be the best you can be is desired, but if you deliberately sabotage others in your quest for glory and without any real reason…Hmm, what makes your life more important than the next?

The next time you wonder – if s/he is worth it, ask yourself if they treat you with respect. Everyone makes mistakes and isn't perfect, but if they are genuine about their feelings, they will make every effort to learn from their mistakes and to treat you as their equal.

Poverty

To judge one
On the things they own
Or the clothes they wear,
When inside, they may be bare;
Their souls are cold and
Their hearts are torn.

What will keep you warm?

I've heard the saying "to punch above one's weight" in regards to males pursuing females they believe are more physically attractive than them and they perceive them to be "out of their league". However, what if that outside layer is purely for show and on the inside, they are empty?

I used to understand that beautiful people would receive attention because we as a species are drawn to things that are pleasant to the eye. But as time goes on, it has become a foreign concept.

When it comes to finding someone that you can be around, their character means so much more than what can be seen. How they make you feel and treat you, what their values are, their direction in life and how well you connect are so much more important.

Sticks and Stones

>Sticks and stones
>May break bones
>But words
>Can scar forever.

What you say to others may impact them forever. Choose your words carefully and if they cannot be kind, it is better to say nothing at all.

Words

Words can be beautiful
Words can be kind
Words can be uplifting
Words can be comforting
Words can be humorous.
But
Words can be destructive
Words can be cruel
Words can be sickening
Words can be confronting
Words can be horrendous.

All that changes them is their sequence. Choose wisely.

Words have the power to create and destroy – which do you choose?

REBOOT

Fog

Months of darkness
Ambling aimlessly
A direction, a purpose –
Nowhere to be found.

Horizon hidden
Behind a fog so dense;
No distinction between
Up or down,
No handle on common sense.

Hibernation, meditation
Required to survive.
Deliberate focus and mindfulness
Muting my goodbye.

A slow, deep breath
Count to ten;
Open up my eyes.
The fog has lifted
A new life I'm gifted;
Thankful I'm alive.

When depression hits and your mind is covered in psychological smog, it is hard to see where you are going, what your life means and you lose the ability to think sensibly.

Mindfulness is useful to centre yourself, remain present and to not let the thoughts that plague your mind take hold. Thoughts are temporary and if you let them pass without being hooked by them, you will soon see the sun again.

Waves

Floating. Drifting. Bobbing.
At the mercy of the swell.
Pulling me left. Pushing me right.
Beating me to the edge of my life.

Hauling me in
Splashing my face;
Covering me in its
Salty embrace.

Spitting me out.
Dragging me down.
Not caring if I live
Or drown.

Ride the waves
Head above the surf;
Let them rise and fall
Until they disperse.

Emotions and thoughts will rise and fall, just as waves. Some will be powerful, some will approach without warning and try to pull you under.

If you try to control the waves by swallowing them, they will drown you. If you are aware of the stories they try to convince you of, you can ride them until them have subsided into a gentle ripple in which you are safe to explore them; with the objective of understanding and learning, not to push them away.

Breathe

Lying on my behind staring at the sky;
Wind is cool, the sun up high
My breathing slows as I
Begin to close my eyes.
Time loses meaning as
My limbs begin to lose feeling.
My mind begins to melt and fly;
A tingle travels up my spine.
Consciousness released from
My cerebrum; I disconnect
From my mind as I find
A place of unbridled freedom.

Free from thought.
Free from fear.
A place of self-healing.
Remain until I find,
A state of mind
That brings back human feeling.

One thing that I found that was my anchor in times of emotional turmoil – when I felt as if all I could do was to curl up in a ball, when the thoughts were taking over and the pain thundered in my chest – was meditation.

I would lay on my back with music and practise mindfulness. I would focus on my body, experience the sensations and then let them be. I would then focus on each thought and emotion and make room for them; letting them pass on in their own time.

If you feel overwhelmed or uncomfortable, I suggest looking into ACT therapy, mindfulness and meditation, as they are extremely helpful.

There Were Times

There were times
That tears fell
From my eyes.
There were times
Where my mind
Would tell me only lies.
There were times
That I couldn't move –
Frozen firmly in place.
There were times
Where I wished
It could be erased.
There were times
That I could
Only embrace pain.
There were times
I didn't want to wake again.

In those times
I felt
Deep inside me
A stirring, a truth –
This wasn't all
It was meant to be.
In those times
I stopped;
I let them pass.
They weren't forever
They weren't my future;
I knew they wouldn't last.

Even when you think you have gotten to the point that you are okay, there will be times where everything is dragged up again and will mess you up once more. It will feel ridiculous and you'll feel weak, as if things shouldn't bother you anymore. However, it's normal.

Those times will pass when they are ready, you just need to remain present and show yourself some compassion. Allow the feelings to come and go on their own.

Beating Heart

My heart beats
In a slow rhythm;
Calm. Controlled.

No more do I feel
The hollow ache
Of loneliness bouncing
Off the emptiness in my chest.
No more do I feel
The claws of destruction
Crushing down on me
Squeezing out all hope.
No more do I feel
The need to convince
Those that do not
Appreciate love.

Calm. Controlled.
In a slow rhythm
My heart still beats.

More

What was
Is no more.
What is
Is much more.

When I was able to re-join living life as a functional human being – contributing to my own wellbeing and that of others, making sound and reasonable decisions and enjoying life – I was able to look back and notice how much has changed. The core aspects of myself were still there – the passion, the integrity, the authenticity – but many of the outer layers had been either removed or modified. I discovered things about myself that I didn't know and also the reasons behind them.

Just because things are different from what you expected, don't let the expectation keep you from enjoying what is. Yes, there may be grief, but afterwards, there will be growth.

Mistakes

Everyone makes mistakes
As we're only human.
Perhaps all it needs
Is a second take.

I've heard people say that things are "too hard" when they fail. Perhaps you are trying to learn a new skill and you keep messing up. Perhaps you gained back all the weight you had lost. Perhaps you made a mistake while giving a speech/ performance. Perhaps you hurt someone you care about.

No one is perfect (something I forget a lot) and we will all stuff up from time to time.

But if the outcome is something you are aiming for, then all you can do is get up, dust yourself off, learn from the mistake and try again. Don't let the fear of past mistakes stop you. Make a plan to beat that weight, keep practising that skill until you master it or put aside blame/ anger/ pride and reach out to those you miss.

Not trying is worse than failing.

Leap

Climb from the rubble
Stand atop the heap,
Find it easier to breathe –
To let go of your troubles;
To take that freeing leap.

When everything you had has been torn down, it gives you the freedom to build again, stronger than before.

Start

It's never too late
It's never too hard
All you need to do
Is make a start.

If you want something, regardless of what it is (okay, as long as it's not intentionally hurting another) you can make it happen.

Want to get fit? Start being more active and change your diet. Want to learn a new skill? Do some investigation and then practise! Miss someone? Reach out to them.

Your mind tells you all kinds of stories (mostly negative) that can keep you stuck. Gain momentum and shut them out and you'll be surprised at how far you go.

Senses

I see the fragility in your smile
I see the shake of your hands
I see the closeness with which
you hold your chest.

I hear the stammer in your speech
I hear the rasp in your breath
I hear the ruffle of your skirt
as you shift in place.

I feel the pain behind your eyes
I feel the doubt plaguing your mind
I feel the fear that grips you tight
eyes flicking left to right.

Being broken is not the end;
Simply a means to start again.

Restart

I wonder
If those that have
Lost their hearts
Know that, in time
It is possible to
Restart?

I remember when I was broken, that I believed that I would never love again; I would be fine on my own and that it would be too hard to try.

How I was wrong.

For all those in the midst of relationship pain, know that if you want it, you will find what you're looking for.

Chain and Anchor

The final link in this chain
To be broken from this anchor
So I may resurface
To breathe once again.

ACTION

Stand

Knock the dirt
Off your soul
Stand back
Upon your feet;
Don't let
A single event
Signal your defeat.

There will be challenges in your life that knock you from your feet, knock you off course and challenge your very core. They will make you question everything; even question your very existence. Don't let them take you down, learn what you need from them and grow.

Open Eyes

Keep an open heart,
an open mind and
Open eyes.

You'll be
Pleasantly surprised
By what you find.

When you reach a point where the things you see, feel or believe no longer make sense to you, they feel foreign and/or make you feel uncomfortable, an option available is to grow and change. Perhaps you've come out of the other side of trauma and you can no longer view the world in the same way.

You have the ability to form a new view, belief and opinion by gathering information, interacting with the environment around you and those in it and observing how it makes you feel. If you remain open to experience, you may come to appreciate things differently from the way you used to.

Listen, Think, Speak

Think before you speak.
Listen before you think.

If you discuss thoughts or ideas without the knowledge behind the idea, it is how rumours, gossip and conspiracy theories are created.

Where does your knowledge come from? If it is purely from what you believe you know? You could be misinformed or your mind may be telling you stories. No one knows everything about everything and the only way to gain further knowledge and a more balanced view is to listen to and share information with others.

Free Thought

Utilise your imagination
Before it's owned by the corporation
Where they request a donation
For its emancipation, or
Become a slave of their designation.

Many people will tell you many things. Some of them useful, many of them not. Each person will have had their own experiences and this shapes their view. Many will be unable to see things from a different perspective.

Learning to live for the things that bring you happiness and peace and not for others is a rewarding and fulfilling existence.

Analyse

Observe. Analyse.
Look for what hides inside.
How does it feel?
Is it something you can't describe?
Is it something real?

Does it bring you comfort?
Does it instil fear instead?
Is it beyond your boundaries?
Is it where you cannot tread?

Are you anxious?
Are you relaxed?
Are you restless?
Are you scared?
How exactly do you feel?

All these things
And many more;
Understanding they will bring;
Show you things
You didn't know before.

When you encounter a situation that is new, instead of running away, be present in the moment and observe it. How does it make you feel? What does it make you think? Is it pushing you to your limits and can you handle it?

Before you run away from a new situation, be present in it.

Why

First, ask why.
Then, ask why again.

To understand
the answer,
Why is your question.

Ask why once more,
Just to be sure.

The final why
Will be the real answer.

When I tried to understand why the actions of another had hurt me so much, to the point where the pain was so great that I couldn't function and no longer wanted to be here, I was given no real information to form an answer.

I couldn't change what had happened. I couldn't stop the pain from occurring. So the only option I had was to try to understand why I was feeling the pain. It wasn't until I went to therapy that I was able to discover the true, root cause of my pain. It went something like this...

Q. Why am I in pain?
A. Because I loved someone that walked out on me.
Q. Why is that causing me pain?
A. Because I believed they loved me as I loved them.
Q. Why is that causing me pain?
A. Because when I asked if that was the case, they said they did.
Q. Why is that causing me pain?
A. Because they weren't completely honest with me and did not have compassion for how I may have been feeling.
Q. Why is that causing me pain?
A. Because I value integrity and I had placed my trust in that person to be honest with me.

That's when it all made sense to me and I was able to move forward. If you never seek to understand the why behind the hurt, you will never find the closure you seek. It may take more or less whys, but eventually it gets to the root cause.

Outside In

When you look
From the outside in
That's when change
Can begin.

When you wish to foster change, looking at yourself from another perspective is required. Step outside of yourself and look at your habits, behaviours, emotions and thoughts. How are they affecting you and what is the effect?

Learning to be able to listen to your thoughts without accepting every single one is a tricky but required step.

Strong

Stand tall
Stand strong
For in this world
Is where you belong.

The shockwave
Will come.
Try to pull you –
Pull everything down
Until you are undone.

Brace yourself
With all your might;
This will be
One hell of a fight.

When you find your feet, when you find your place, there will be many who will be confused and/or upset. They will question you, belittle you, tempt you and taunt you. They are scared that you have found your strength and that they can no longer influence you.

Be prepared.

Fear Fuel

Face your fears.
Crush them.
Burn them.
Use them as fuel.

Fear holds everyone in place in regards to something. Use that fear to fuel you, to drive you and as motivation to achieve your goals.

Succeed

Put in your everything
Put in your all;
When you've got nothing
Give even more.

You'll be called crazy
You'll be called stupid;
At least you'll know
You've contributed.

Don't ever give in
Don't ever give up;
Even when they
Tell you to stop.

For they are the naysayers
They are the jealous;
Don't want you to be
Something momentous.

Do what it takes
Do what you need
To get to the end;
Make sure you succeed.

There are many negative people in this world who have been told how to live and what to do. They feel they should then force this upon others, to make sure they do not become better than them.

If you work hard and put in effort, you'll be called crazy, you'll be called stupid, but when you achieve your goals, you can say you made it, regardless of their doubt.

Fake

Fake is the new black
Pretend your life is 'perfect'
Hide the undesirable
Under the surface
Until the façade becomes
Cracked.

Fake nails.
Fake tales.
Fake hair.
Fake care.
Fake interaction.
Fake introspection.
Fake personality.
Fake sincerity.
Fake patience.
Fake relationships.

In a world of fake
Don't be one of the sheep,
Be yourself and take the leap,
Go for that first step
That others are
Too afraid to take.

There are so many people pretending to be someone they aren't, even if they realise it or not. Don't be afraid to be yourself, even if you feel you don't "fit in"; being happy and content in your own skin is a big step that most are too afraid to even attempt.

Finding your own sense of happiness is rewarding and brings a huge sense of satisfaction and freedom. Find out who you are and what your values are and see what happens.

Leaves

As they fall from atop the trees
Tumble down,
Gracefully and with ease.
One atop the other upon the ground
Collect these multicolour leaves.

They gather together
They snuggle up;
The flow of travel they disrupt.
When the wind whips
They scatter and disperse;
Carried away
In an invisible hearse.

Watch them twist
Watch them fly;
Smile at them
Whilst waving goodbye.
For they shall go far,
They shall go wide;
Shan't trouble you
On the inside.

Dr. Russ Harris describes letting go of troubling thoughts in a metaphor about leaves – imagine the problem or feeling you are having as a leaf, sitting in the palm of your hand. Look at it, examine it, learn from it. Do not try to throw it away, but let the wind carry it away when it's ready.

I found this description and exercise to be amazingly beneficial in handling thoughts of depression and anxiety. This poem is my description of this idea; leaves can pile up and block your path. If you let them naturally blow away, they will be scattered and no longer in your way.

Focus

Did you know –
There's more to life than
Broken hearts
Tear stained pillows and
Empty ice cream cups.
There's also –
Magnificent sunsets
Stupendous silence and
Never-ending wonder.

You just need to know
Where to focus.

If you are so deeply buried in your misery, you'll miss the serenity when it's in plain view, for all to see.

Pressure

With the right pressure and heat
You can turn this ash back to gems
Until one day, you shine bright again.

When you reach rock bottom and it seems everything is against you, take a moment to breathe. Things are not as they may seem. Focus on the internal and ignore the outward world; allow yourself to heal and grow. You'll be surprised at how far you can go.

DEFINING

Define

What makes you smile?
What brings you joy?
What are the activities
You cannot ignore?

What makes you angry?
What makes you cry
What atrocities
Make you die inside?

What drives you?
What do you stand for?
Where do your dreams lead,
What must you pursue?

What fills your soul?
What makes your heart ring?
What are the moments
That make you whole?

These are the aspects
That are your design.
It is time for you
To define.

Working out who you are makes it easier to go to where you need to be.

Chase Your Happiness

The longer you spend
Chasing someone
else's dream
The further away
Happiness will seem.

Figure out what makes you happy and then do it. Your definition of happiness will be different to everyone else. When you are doing what makes you happy, others will notice and they'll become happier too.

Who Are You?

Align your actions.
Birth your beliefs.
Clarify your calling.
Define your direction.
Expose your emotions.
Fortify your feelings.
Generate your goals.
Hone your honesty.
Ignite your integrity.
Pursue your passions.
Verify your values.

For once you do
You shall be true.

Time is Money

Time, like money,
Has value.
Only you
Can decide their worth.

You wouldn't deliberately throw your money into the fire and watch it burn; so why spend time doing things that bring you down instead of building you up?

Spending hours of time lost in the fog and not being present is life wasted. Practise mindfulness and connect with the world around you.

Me, Myself and I

The more you live
To please others
The less of yourself
You will discover.

If you are living a lie; pretending to be someone else for the sake of others, eventually you will run out of steam. No one can pretend forever. Not only is it stressful, it can eventually affect your health if it is for a prolonged period.

Also, if you are doing things because you feel you are in someone's debt, stop and think about how you are interacting with the world around you; is it what you really want? Is it who you really want to be? If you feel uncomfortable for some reason, perhaps you are living too much for someone else, rather than for yourself.

Limits

Where is the edge
What is your peak;
Have you found the answer
To what makes you weak?

What makes you cringe
What makes you cry?
Those experiences that
Make you question why.

How far can you go
Where will you stop?
When will it all
Become a little too much.

Are you giving
Your everything, your all
But you feel yourself
Against the wall?

Those are your limits
That is your end;
But when you fall,
You must get up
And try all over again.

How can you know what is too much if you have never reached your end? When you have reached a point where you feel like you cannot give anymore, even though you have to? When you define your limits, that is when you can redefine them.

Ponder the Path

When I look
At those following
The 'normal' path
I sit and ponder
What's at the end?

What are you doing with your journey?

Personal

Only for me
Never for you.

I write to express ideas and to help people realise they are not alone in their thoughts/emotions, to inspire others and to help bring change in society. I do not write to gain acceptance to have people like me. Every time I have people that sell some form of recognition contact me, I ignore and block them. There's no integrity in buying acceptance. The same with personal actions, live by your values, not for acceptance.

Yours

I'll live my life
Just this way
If you don't like it
Get out of my way.

People will judge your actions, your motives, choices and your very character; but it doesn't impact upon their state of mind at the end of the day. Be true to your core values so you may smile widely, laugh loudly and sleep peacefully.

Your Mountain

When you stand atop the mountain,
Looking down into the valley,
What do you see?

A thriving village
Of all those
Most important to you.
Fishing in the river,
Lazing in the sun;
Playing peacefully.

Or is it pristine,
a clear, blue lake.
A small wooden hut.
Just you, and nature.
As the wind whips
Between the trees.

Or perhaps a metropolis,
A bustling hub
Of leaders and believers.
Determined and driven,
Devoting their energy
To bring about societal change.

When you climb your mountain,
Look down into your valley,
What will you see?

When you look back at your life and all the things you have accomplished, what do you want to see? An empire, a family, a humble life? What goals do you want to complete and why? How do they align with your values?

Ensure that your climb to the peak is not wasted.

Perfect Fit

It's not settling,
It's learning
What brings you joy
And ignoring
What others
Tell you to enjoy.

There will always be people on the outside who will judge you, your relationship, your life and your partner. They will say they "aren't enough x" or "too y". However, that is their opinion.

As they aren't you and ultimately, their opinions will have little to no impact on your life. Don't let their opinions change the way you feel; by all means, use their input to help form your own decisions, but do not give them power in your life.

Jealousy, envy and greed are strong motivations in some people; be wary of them.

Puzzle

Pieces placed face down,
Curves twist and colours gone.
No way to tell
Right from wrong.

Impossible to start,
To tell them apart;
But if you begin at an edge
You'll come out ahead.

It might be relaxing,
Find joy in the sorting.
No need for frustration
If you enjoy exploring.

Examine each individual piece,
Finger every curve and slope;
Are they jagged? Are they smooth?
Are they filled with hope?

These piece fit in a single way;
Only in one puzzle, not another.
To force it to fit,
Would lead to disarray.

Discover the edges,
Discover the flaws;
For this life puzzle
Can only be yours.

Life can be confusing as hell and you may ask a lot of people for advice about what to do, where do I fit, what's my purpose…but at the end of the day, it's your life and you have to live with the consequences of your actions. Do not let another's opinions dictate your choices. Do what feels right. Do what fits.

Room

Four white walls
and a polished floor.
No cupboards.
No room to hoard.

Dust may gather
But doesn't stay long,
A brief visit
Before it moves along.

The room begins to fill
The floor covered in piles
Daylight blocked.
The room feels stifled.

Boxes must be opened
Their contents reviewed;
Remove the waste and junk.
Time and space to be renewed.

Those memories and items I wish to keep
Place gently, stacked neatly inside.
Now a tiny pile
That defines my life.

Carrying all the belonging, memories and people that have ever been in your life along with you forever is tiring. Are they actually bringing or giving you anything worthwhile? Does it add to your happiness? Not everyone or everything you come across in your life is meant to be there forever.

Sometimes letting go is needed; regardless of how close they may have been.

Take Aim and Release

Scan the horizon
Acquire your target.
Select your arrow,
Take aim and release.

You may misfire
It may slip.
It may hit the dirt and skip.
Select your next arrow,
Take aim and release.

Each shot getting closer
as you increase your aim.
When you hit your mark
In jubilation you will exclaim.

Don't stop there –
Select your next arrow,
Breathe deep
Take aim and release.

When you define your values and the goals you wish to achieve in your life, the next step is to align your actions with them so that you are moving towards achieving them.

Initially, you may fall short and fail dismally, but you have to reach into your quiver of motivation and take another shot. Giving up is not an option, as if you give up trying to achieve your goals and align with your values, you are giving up on yourself.

You are the only person who cares about what happens to you and has the power to make a difference. Don't stop taking aim at where you want to be.

MOTIVATE

No Excuse

I'm not a recluse;
The way I spend
My time is
No excuse.

There are times when people won't see me for extended periods of time and this is not by accident. I used to think that I was extremely extroverted, but as time goes on, I've also found that I enjoy my own space and peace and quiet. I don't hide away to avoid others and I don't do it because I don't enjoy their company, it's just that I need quiet to allow myself to feel centred.

How do you centre yourself? Do you have a place that you like to sit at or an activity that you enjoy? When/ how do you feel most comfortable?

Hide and Seek

If you do not value
The things for which you seek
Forever they will remain
Hidden, and out of reach.

If you think about the things you searched for in another or working to create or find in yourself, think about how much you value them. For example, if you wish to be fit and strong, do you eat the right food and perform the appropriate training? Do you wish to become better at a skill and practise to increase your ability? Do you wish to have a solid and respectful relationship, yet do you scoff at those with loyalty?

How aligned are your actions to your values?

Try

If you do not try
You'll continue asking why
Until the very day you die.

1. Work out what brings you happiness and joy.
2. Work on it until you get there.

If you fail, at least you tried and you won't ever wonder if you tried hard enough.

Dive

        Don't live your life
        Splashing in the shallows

        Dive deep to the depths;
        All it takes is one breath.

Worse

 Not trying
 Is worse
 Than failing.

Shoot

Step up to the line.
Look up at the goal.
Steady yourself.
Take the shot.

If you stand at the line of opportunity and never take the shot, you may as well not stand at the line. Even if you miss, at least you tried and have the ability to shoot again.

Remember

Things could be better;
However –
Things could be worse.
Live in the here. Live in the now.
For you're not yet in a hearse.

While we are running around, living our lives and trying to get everything done, it is easy to forget what we have and focus on what we do not.

Take a moment out and just stop and enjoy the fact that you are alive and breathing. Shut out the thoughts and just be; just for a moment.

Never is Forever

If you stay
Afraid of forever
What you long for
You'll find never.

Don't be afraid to take a chance, to take a risk, even when it seems unlikely, for even if you fail, it would be worse to never try.

Reality

Why escape
Your current reality
When only you
Can create
Your new reality?

I see pictures, posts, commercials of people running from their lives, trying to numb their reality. Yes, pain is scary. Yes, pain isn't fun. But by running away, where does this get you?

Why not lay the road of where you want to be rather than running from where you are.

Follow

Wherever your
heart leads
Ensure your
mind follows.

Be present in your life. Whatever you are doing, live in the moment. Do you have someone that loves you? Cherish them. Do you have a hobby/passion which brings you happiness? Engage in it. Are you currently in nature? Look up.

Try not to become bogged down by the pressures of life and open your senses to the world and life around you.

Passion

                    Without passion
                    Why persist?

Whatever you do, make sure to do it with all of you.

Pass It On

Show passion.
Be called crazy.
Pass on the passion;
Make them crazy too.

So many people go through life without any willpower, no driving force, no motivation. When they meet you, make them see your passion and be so infected that they become passionate too.

There are enough living zombies in this world. Don't be one of them.

Zombie Life

Do not be a zombie
Staggering across
The surface of the earth
Stumbling on your way
From day to day.
Define your worth
You'll no longer be lost;
Instead, engaged and living wholly.

Do you remember being a child, full of excitement and wonder, with plans for your future? Do you remember when those around you told you to grow up? Do you remember the moment when you were broken and the harsh realities of "life" were thrust upon you like a coat that is too big and heavy and were told you'd "grow into it." Growing stronger shoulders is not for harbouring the world's problems and to stop living. Growing stronger is for the ability to be aware of the problems in this world and still be you. To not let them blow out the light that is you.

There are so many negative people in this world, ready to knock you down and make sure you stay there so that they don't have any competition. Stand strong and put in that passion that you once had.

Only you can extinguish the flame inside you. Do not let someone else have that much power over you.

Go

Go!
Go for what you want.
Go with everything you have.
Go towards a better life.
Go when others say stop.

Don't let negativity pull you down.
Don't let obstacles stand in your way.
Don't overthink a situation.
Don't talk yourself out of an experience.

Just Go!

Gamble

While the majority are too afraid
To bare their naked soul
Go for broke and risk it all
Send out all you have
And receive whatever is returned;
Be open and completely true.

For even though it may break you
At least you saw it through.

Be the exception to the rule.

Believe

Don't for a second
Believe your life
Is a waste.
We all matter,
You just need
To believe.

If you find yourself in a situation where you feel as if you have accomplished nothing, aren't contributing, feel stuck or desire direction, do not despair. You will be surprised at the things you have achieved so far and the things you could achieve, if you just believe in yourself.

If you are at the bottom, wondering if you should continue living, never ever give up. You can make an impact, you can rebuild and succeed, only if you believe it. Don't let the negativity of others control your life, your mind, your happiness. Be your own captain and direct your life where you want to go.

ALIGN

Wrongs and Rights

Use the wrongs
To make rights.

There are many things that can cause trauma in this world. When you have the strength, use that strength to help lift others out of the fog and into the sunlight.

Complimenting

Stop complaining;
Start complimenting.

If your focus is centred on how the world is against you, your view will be skewed to notice the negative. Instead, look for the positive. Notice the good that is your life and in the world around you.

Inspire those around you to cultivate more positivity.

Perfectly Imperfect

Use your imperfections
To paint your picture
As no one can be
Perfectly imperfect
As you.

True Colours

My true colours
Are drawn upon me
In shades of grey.

Passion – giving all that I've got.
Integrity – doing what is right,
regardless of what they say.
Authentic – Not pretending
to be what I'm not.

This is something very important to me because there are so many (the majority) people who never show their true selves. Always trying to fit in with others when then know it's not them and feeling uncomfortable because of it.

What they don't realise is that by being themselves, they will discover an amazing freedom that will make them happier than they have ever been.

Remains

>Beauty shall fade
>Integrity and
>authenticity
>All that shall
>remain.

PIA

Passion. Integrity. Authentic. How I live my life.

People. Internal. All. Make peace with others, within yourself and your environment.

Patience. Infinite. Acceptance. Having the ability to be patient, accept what is and do so without falter.

Perceive. Interrogate. Accept. Understand what is going on around you, ask why and accept it.

Pare. Inconsiderable. Amiable. Remove the things from your life which aren't helpful, don't worry about the things you cannot control and always be kind.

Promote. Interact. Applaud. Encourage people, talk with them and acknowledge them for their contribution.

Possibility. Instigate. Achieve. Think of what you can do, put it into action and follow through.

Personality. Intelligence. Attractiveness. Personality and intelligence are also forms of attractiveness, not just physical beauty.

Positive. Impromptu. Approachable. Be a positive person, who can be spontaneous, flexible and someone who people can interact with without worrying about how you will perceived by them.

People in Action. All of these lead to people that can contribute to society in a positive way that benefits everyone in a selfless manner.

I am working at this every day and I am only human and there are times when I fail. But deep down, my intentions are pure; I only want the best for people and for them to be the best they can be. If everyone worked together, life would be an easier experience.

Treasure

She uncovered
insecurities
Deep in my heart.
As she removed them
From my sunken chest,
She held them tenderly,
Called them treasures
As she buffed them
and put them on display.

Kind

Always be kind
For you cannot
Read another's mind.

One of the things that I have learnt and experienced personally is that you can never truly know what someone else is thinking, no matter how well you know them. They may be experiencing trauma and hardships that you know nothing about.

By treating people with respect and kindness, you are more likely to receive an open and positive response. If they respond with negativity, don't take it personally, but instead consider their response with compassion and try to understand what they may be going through.

If more people did this, there would be less miscommunication and frustration in this world.

Sunshine and Landmines

If another's path
Crossed yours
Or perhaps they
intertwine;
If it's forever
Or only a short while,
Make theirs beautiful.
Plant flowers and dance
in the sunshine.
Don't litter their way
With rubble and landmines.

You will meet many people in your life. Some will be there forever, some only a brief while but they will all shape your path. Whatever their purpose, aim to treat them as you would yourself and have a positive impact, rather than a detrimental one.

Destruction and pain are much harder to repair compared to providing growth.

Kindness

Kindness
Is free
But its value
Is greater
than any
Commodity.

Doing something for someone, based purely on being able to make the life of someone else easier and NOT what you can receive for it is true kindness. EVERYONE is battling demons that we know nothing about. How about lending a hand to your fellow man and lighten the load, just a little? Even just a hello and a smile can be a welcome change in someone's day. Kindness is that rare now that people confuse it with flirtation.

Be someone that looks for that opportunity to help another and help spread kindness.

HULK

This world
Will always
Need more
Kindness.

Not only does the world need more kindness, but it needs Honesty, Understanding and Love. These are things everyone needs. These are easy enough to give to the people you know and care about, but to emit these things to everyone, every day, is difficult. Why?

Perhaps you feel uncomfortable interacting with people you don't know or you feel it's "unfair" as you won't receive anything in return.

At its core, every action we take is motivated to satisfy some internal driver. Instead, put yourself in the other person's shoes and think about if you were to receive such interactions from someone else, how would it make you feel?

Worth

You worth is not measured
In dollars and cents,
But in integrity,
Kindness and common sense.

Project and Attract

Project
Kindness and
positivity
And watch your
environment
Change into
your fantasy.

Probably the biggest change I've noticed in myself is my attitude towards people and society. I used to be judgemental (without reason or realising!) and it would make me a bit jealous and cynical. Now that I've taken a step back and learnt things about life, I understand more about how things are and how little I know. I feel quite humble in comparison to who I was.

One thing I do know, is that being positive towards others, and offering kindness is something that everyone needs. I try my best to be positive towards everyone, but I fail at times. However, understanding that everyone has bad days makes it easier to regroup and try again.

No More

There is
No need
For greed.

Why does human kind strive for more? More possessions, more beauty, more youth, more money, more freedom, more space, more travel, more respect, more EVERYTHING.

Unfortunately, we, as a species, have progressed very little from the days of our cavemen ancestors. They had a true need for more; more shelter, more sustenance, more protection, more people. But we have surpassed that time. We aren't being chased by wild beasts, for we have developed weapons to kill them and their habitat. Our needs are clearly met, but our minds have yet to evolve and understand this.

Being present, accepting what is and appreciating what you have go a long way to finding your happiness. Don't get caught in the game of impressing others. Impress yourself and become the person whom lives by their values and passions.

Reality

Don't let the voices in your head
Trick you into believing you're worthless;
That it's your true reality instead.
The world may be cold and
people may be heartless;
But a world without souls that feel?
Well, that would be disastrous.

The thoughts you have and the emotions you feel may not be the true reality. Don't let them run rampant without keeping them in check.

Rare

Let me show you
All the things
This world is
Running out of.

Respect

Never expect
Respect;
You must give
Before you
Receive.
Yet, do not accept
Neglect;
No one is bigger
Than they seem.

There is always a lot of talk about respect, especially within relationships and mostly it seems to directed at men. A belief that we, as a gender, are not well versed at showing respect to those in our lives.

However, respect is not a one way street; it requires both people to give as much as they receive. Not showing appreciation for your partner or not communicating with them makes it difficult to receive respect if you don't give it in return.

Respect those around you as you respect yourself and notice the difference in their response.

Leigh Gembus

The Gentleman

The gentleman: a rarity; a dying breed.
A patient, caring man – solid and dependable
Always there in times of duress, to support and cater to every need.
An upstanding citizen, morals to uphold
Witness and victim of cases of injustice
His kind and positive nature won't fold.

A considerate man, burning with passion
Driven by his desires, following callings that have meaning
Whilst keeping others in mind. Sharing his time and life
With all those around; conveying his compassion.
Respects every woman and man – all created the same
Everyone on a personal journey
None that stops them from saying his name.

That being said, he isn't a fool; a pushover? Untrue.
Stands up for his beliefs without using fists
But instead with the brain that fills his head.
Unafraid to laugh at himself, for life is fun
Share the happiness. Let the love run.
All things in jest – no harm done.
Aware of himself, big headed he is not
Being honest and open are virtues that he's got.

Commands an audience when entering a room
Not through attention seeking stunts executed obnoxiously.
Manners and language of the highest class
A firm handshake and his warmth extend exponentially.
Gives his full attention during any conversation
Responds quickly without hesitation
Without imposing his personal view.

The gentleman – dapper in his fitted suit
His hygiene proper; not a hair out of place.
Noticed by women; proclaiming – "he's cute".
Knows his worth, in control of his personal space
Energetic and enthusiastic – spinning yarns
Laughter echoes; reaches the climax without egg on his face.

The greatest measure of a gentleman
Is his treatment of the women in his life
Knowing their importance, displays the upmost respect.
Refrains from playing them against one another
His heart and desire run in parallel together.
Can't question his words or actions

Acts as if each is his wife.

However, mistakes he will make
Apologetic and admitting fault
Rectifying them as best he can;
For everyone's sake.

When meeting someone new
Positivity and respect shine through
Giving his attention and looking in her eyes
Without giving her the once over
Or thinking solely of what lies between her thighs.
Ask questions, comes to know who she is
Interested in the woman behind the beautiful face
Slow, controlled, measured and understanding
That's the pace that will win this important race.

When he is ready and finds the right one
Eternal outpouring of love and emotion will have begun.
Always puts her first, no matter the case;
A solid, dependable rock to come home to
Love and support stands unwavering in place.
Loyal to just one; protective without smothering
They understand one another; they communicate
So they will never become undone.
However their language isn't just through the words they speak
A purer form of communication when their bodies meet.
No fears, no worries when they are face to face
No words required, engulfed in burning passion
Their desires require no explanation.
Lay intertwined for hours until they sleep
Where in their dreams they will once again meet.

This my friends are some aspects of a gentleman
A man worthy of your time.
Keep him close to you; right by your side.
For he may not admit it openly
However, he is grateful for you all
Happiness abundant on the inside
Gives him the strength to stand tall.

Reputation

When people
speak my name
I don't want them to
Be excited because
They know of me
But because
They know of my character.

Let your reputation precede you.

When You're Dead

As you lay
On satin sheets
In your sharpest suit
Surrounded by those
Nearest and dearest,
What words will they speak
When you're dead?

Will they speak
Of your riches and beauty
Of your mansion and rhinoplasty
Of your likes and followers
Of your clothes and helicopter?
Or
Will they speak
Of your love and your heart
Of your passion and smarts
Of your kindness and integrity
Of your empathy and authenticity?

I know which words
I would choose
To leave in my stead.

What REALLY matters?

REFLECT

Wisdom

Wisdom is knowing
You don't know.

The more that you experience, the more you learn and begin to understand. Eventually you get to a point where you realise that there is so much that you DON'T know, it's kind of frightening. That's when the fun begins; as you investigate and learn about the things that are interesting and important to you.

Always be open to different perspectives as it allows you to add to your knowledge and make connections between things you've never considered before.

Never dismiss information (unless you can prove it is invalid) as you never know when it could come in handy.

Yesterday

Yesterday
You said
You no longer
Wanted us.

Today
I stand tall
And leave you
In my dust.

It's funny how time changes things; one day things seem bright before they come crashing down. The brightness only returns when you decide to open the door again.

Leigh Gembus

Ruins

I have to dig deep
In the ruins of love lost
To remember the pain
That once held me in chains.

I remember days where I could barely move, I didn't eat, I didn't sleep and my mind was filled with nightmares, whether I was asleep or awake.

I was so lost in the haze of pain where there times that I seriously considered ending my life.

I used to wonder if those days would ever end; if I could ever return to a place where I would be able to smile and laugh and not feel the pain that would be closing in around me from all directions.

The answer is yes, it does end – if you want it to. You have to want to be free from the pain to get there. How? Time, patience, kindness, acceptance of yourself, emotions and thoughts and being present in your life all help you get to the point where you can live again, and finally – when you are ready – forgiveness.

Don't give up fighting, because things can turn around. You have to want it.

(Passing in the) Stillness of Time

Here is where I exist.
The pain no longer persists.

When it bubbles and flares,
I remain still;
It shall pass.

I no longer live the
nightmare.

The old saying of time heals all would is true (to an extent, of course). The amount of time that it takes you to get to a place of peace will vary for everyone; it's your journey and your emotions – pretending to be in a place that you are not ready to be in will bring more pain.

Take the time you need. However, do not wallow in the pain. If you remain focused on the person/situation, it will bring up all the pain afresh. You cannot heal if you remain connected to what hurts you.

There will be times when it will enter your mind, but by being mindful of yourself, knowing that it will pass and not trying to control it by pushing it away, you will find the relief you desire.

Time

Time
Is of
Human
Design.

It doesn't measure
How deeply you loved
Or
How devastating the loss
Or
How hard you laughed
Or
How jagged the scars.

It's purely a measure
Of how long ago
These moments
Have passed.
Nothing more.

Existed

If I try to recall
The person I was
Just a few years ago
The memories are lost;
It's like he never
Existed at all.

It's funny how time changes things, but it's good how time brings out your best if you let it.

Existence

Memories
Of my former self
A distant star.

Light years ago;
Sputtering.
Glowing.
Fluttering.
Going.

Their light so dim
Even I question
Their existence.

Hope

To those that –
Have had their heart
Wrenched from within,
Have had their trust
Slashed and singed,
Have had their hope
Dashed and deflated,
Have had their love
Crucified and confiscated –

There IS hope to be found
You just need to allow
Yourself time to heal
Until once again you can feel.

A lot of writers I follow seem to have been through the same experiences as I; but I can say that if you want to move past those that have treated you unfairly or situations that have changed you, you can, if you want to.

Forgiveness

To grow
One must forgive.
To let go and move past
Whatever they did.

It's not for them,
It is for you;
The power is yours –
See what it can do.

Forgiveness is tricky
It can be hard.
It may take a few tries
For it to finally stick.

But the benefits are endless
I hope you will see;
Holding onto pain
Is not meant to be.

Forgiving those that have hurt you can be one of the hardest things in the world to do, but for you to move past what they may have done to you is necessary, for your own state of mind. Holding onto pain and suffering only hurts you, no one else.

It may seem that the pain is too great and it would be and it would be impossible for you to forgive, but with time, the pain will subside. The anger will fade. By allowing yourself to forgive, you allow positive emotions to enter your mind and focus on the things that build you, not break you.

Open Hearted

A
Heart broken
Is a
Heart opened.

If you've had your heart broken, you know how much you begin to feel. You have never felt emotions so intensely as you do now. You have never cherished moments as much as you do now. You have never given back as much as you do now. You have never lived as much as you do now.

One of the best things about being torn asunder is how much more deeply you experience everything. It brings you alive. Once the pain subsides, everything is richer. Share it with others and help them to engage more too.

Dreams to Reality

My future no longer
An oasis; shimmering
In the distance.
With each step,
Each new day,
My dreams
Are becoming
My reality.

Parade

I've had people
Stand in my way;
Now it's time
For them to
Stand to the side
Of my parade.

There will always be people who don't want to see you succeed, either because they are jealous, they see you as a threat or they envy you. Don't let them deter you, remain true to yourself and your goals and see them through until you succeed.

Once Again

>Once you've arrived
>At your destination
>Don't forget from
>Where you came;
>Remain humble
>For you may
>End up back there
>Once again.

When you feel that you have yourself worked out, don't sit and wave it in front of others and ridicule them for not having it together; remember that you too, were once there and in the blink of an eye, you could be back there. Help others to help themselves and they will be there when you call their name.

What Have I Learnt From a Broken Heart?

I learnt that people
Are selfish and proud.
To their own wellbeing
They are devout.

I learnt everything changes
It never stays the same.
A million different reasons,
A single one not to blame.

I learnt the power
Of my mind;
The depths of my abilities
Only it can define.

I learnt to love
After heartbreaking pain.
Once you love yourself
Your heart will open again.

I learnt compassion;
To understand and be kind,
Everyone has similarities
That are easy to find.

I learnt to sing,
I found my voice;
I learnt you always
Have a choice.

But most of all
I learnt
We cannot close our eyes
For the day we do
We begin our demise.

Life is a crazy journey for everyone. If you remain blind to your experiences, if you do not question the world around you or seek to understand, you will not learn, grow or evolve. If you decide to live your life based on the actions, thoughts or beliefs of others, you will find yourself in a place where you are uncomfortable and do not know how to be yourself. Discover, learn and question yourself to discover who you truly are. Only then can you align your actions with your values and discover a life you are truly happy to live in.

ABOUT THE AUTHOR

Leigh Gembus has been actively writing poetry for the past four years; using his experiences to create pieces that resonate with others. His writing shines a light on different aspects of life that are not always obvious. For more of Leigh's writing, please go to his Instagram page (@submeg), his ETSY shop (https://www.etsy.com/au/shop/Submeg) or his website (http://submeg.com/).

www.ingramcontent.com/pod-product-compliance
Lightning Source LLC
Chambersburg PA
CBHW071909290426
44110CB00013B/1337